Under the Moon
& Over the Sea

Acknowledgements

The editor and publisher gratefully acknowledge permission to use the following material:

"Once the Wind" © Shake Keane; "Flying Fish" reprinted by kind permission of John Agard c/o Caroline Sheldon Literary Agency; "Emily Hurricane" © Alan Smith; "El Dorado" © Maggie Harris; The poem "Swimmer" is taken from the book Once Upon an Animal published by Bloomsbury Children's Books 1998, by Faustin Charles; "Seashell" reproduced with permission of The Peters Fraser & Dunlop Group Limited © James Berry; "Aximu's Awakening" © 1983 Pamela Mordecai. First used in New Island Readers Book 1, Collins Educational 1983. Used by permission of the poet and the HSW Literary Agency; "Old World New World" reprinted by kind permission of John Agard c/o Caroline Sheldon Literary Agency; "I like to stay up" reproduced with permission of Curtis Brown Ltd, London, on behalf of Grace Nichols © Grace Nichols 1988 & 1994; "Duppy Dan" reprinted by kind permission of John Agard c/o Caroline Sheldon Literary Agency; "Jumbie Man" © Faustin Charles; "Ebbeeleewee" © Faustin Charles; "Anancy" reprinted by permission of Lillian Allen from Nothing but a Hero, published by Well Versed/Woman's Press, Toronto, Canada © 1990; "Mama-Wata" reproduced with permission of Curtis Brown Ltd, London, on behalf of Grace Nichols © Grace Nichols 1988 & 1994; "Jamaican Song" Reproduced with permission of The Peters Fraser Dunlop Group Limited © James Berry; "Listen" © Telcine Turner; "Who U?" © Marc Matthews; "Humming-bird" © reprinted by kind permission of Jessica Huntley c/o Bogle–L'Ouverture Publications Limited; "Listening to the Land" from Poems of Succession by Martin Carter, published by New Beacon Books 1977; "Listening for Answers" ("Why?") © Aimee Harris-Watmore; "Tell Me Trees! What Are You Whispering?" © Wilson Harris; "Poinciana Passion" © Cheryl A. P. Albury from Perspectives from Inner Windows; "Six O'Clock Feeling" © Kamal Singh; "I Love Johnnie Bake" and "Hungry Girl" © John Lyons, first published in Hello New! by Orchard Books; "Guidance" © 2000 Valerie Bloom. Originally published by Bloomsbury Children's Books; "Fruit in a Bowl" © A. J. Seymour from A. J. Seymour: Collected Poems 1927-1989; "Pawpaw" © Kamau Braithwaite; "Windrush Child" (for Vince Reid, the youngest passenger on the Windrush – he was thirteen at the time). Reprinted by kind permission of John Agard c/o Caroline Sheldon Literary Agency; "I Love Me Mudder" © from Wicked World by Benjamin Zephaniah (Puffin, 2000). Text © Benjamin Zephaniah, 2000. Illustrations © Sarah Symonds, 2000. Reproduced by permission of Penguin Books Ltd.; "My Gran Visits England" Reproduced with permission of Curtis Brown Ltd, London, on behalf of Grace Nichols © Grace Nichols 1988 & 1994; "Goodbye Granny" from Singing Down the Breadfruit by Pauline Stewart, published by Bodley Head. Used by permission of The Random House Group Limited; "De" reproduced by permission of the author, from Let Me Touch the Sky by Valerie Bloom, first published by Macmillan Children's Books 2000; "Making My First Snowman" Reproduced with permission of Curtis Brown Ltd, London, on behalf of Grace Nichols © Grace Nichols 1988 & 1994; "The Names That Ran Away" © Kwame Dawes, reprinted by permission of Kwame Dawes; "Occasion" reprinted with permission of The Peters Fraser and Dunlop Group Limited © James Berry.

Every effort has been made to secure permission for the use of copyrighted material. If notified of any omission, the editor and publisher will gladly make the necessary correction in future printings.

First published 2002 by Walker Books Ltd, 87 Vauxhall Walk, London SE11 5HJ

This edition published 2003   10 9 8 7 6 5 4 3 2 1

Poems © individual authors as noted in Acknowledgements
Illustrations © 2002 Cathie Felstead, Jane Ray, Christopher Corr, Satoshi Kitamura, Sara Fanelli

British Library Cataloguing in Publication Data:
a catalogue record for this book is available from the British Library

ISBN 0-7445-9842-7

www.walkerbooks.co.uk

Under the Moon
&
Over the Sea

A Collection of Caribbean Poems

Edited by

John Agard & Grace Nichols

Illustrated by

Cathie Felstead

Jane Ray

Christopher Corr

Satoshi Kitamura

Sara Fanelli

WALKER BOOKS
AND SUBSIDIARIES
LONDON · BOSTON · SYDNEY

Contents

Coral beaches. Cactus-sheltered bays. Winds racing from the Atlantic to meet granite rock. Mysterious drawings left by Carib Indians whose name lives on in the islands of the Caribbean and whose canoes sailed this blue-green sea long, long before the ships of Columbus. Before the infamous slave ships and pirate ships. What secrets lie under the waves of the sea? What treasures are stored in its depths? That's for the sea to know and for all to wonder.

ONCE THE WIND SAID TO THE SEA

CREOLE PROVERB

If you go to crab dance
you mus' get mud

Traditional

ONCE THE WIND

Once the wind
said to the sea
I am sad
      And the sea said
Why
      And the wind said
Because I
am not blue like the sky
or like you

      So the sea said what's
so sad about that

      Lots
of things are blue
or red or other colours too
      but nothing
neither sea nor sky
can blow so strong
or sing so long as you

      And the sea looked sad
      So the wind said
Why

Shake Keane

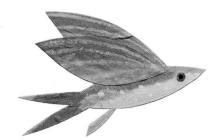

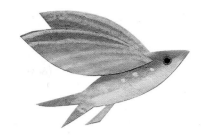

FLYING FISH

Flying fish
flying fish
what is your wish?

In water
you swim
yet like to skim
through wind

Flying fish
flying fish
make up your mind

Are you a bird
inside a fish
or just a fish
dreaming of wings?

John Agard

13

EMILY HURRICANE

Woke up this morning
to a breakfast sky,
fed the kitten marmalade,
had some sunshine in my tea
and then went out to greet the day,
met Miss Emily Hurricane.

She said
Wouldn't you like to swim in the sky,
sail with the trees as they go whizzing by,
dance with the rooftops as they go bubbling?
Wouldn't you like to swim in the sky?

She had silver hair
but it was kind of wild,
electricity for eyes
and a crackling laugh,
ranting and raving
like she was crazy.

She kept singing to me
Wouldn't you like to swim in the sky,
sail with the trees as they go whizzing by,
dance with the rooftops as they go bubbling?
Wouldn't you like to swim in the sky?

I asked her,
"Why are you howling
outside my windows?"
She answered,
"Rounding up beaches to herd away
and deliver to a better place."

And the beaches like white sheep but sad,
their beauty blemished with tar and debris,
were elated to run away with her
and find a safer home at the bottom of the sea.

As they left she whistled,
Wouldn't you like to swim in the sky,
sail with the trees as they go whizzing by,
dance with the rooftops as they go bubbling?
Wouldn't you like to swim in the sky?

I shouted in reply,
"Maybe someday I'd like to join the beaches
at the bottom of the sea."
As she disappeared I heard her sing,
"If you ever make it to the bottom of the sea
you can join us as we dance, the beaches and me."

Alan Smith

15

PULLIN' SEINE

Splash!	Afternoon tide roll on.
Heave!	Fishermen pullin' seine.
Come on!	Jasmine pulls me along.
Grab!	de nets like we big and strong.
Sink!	our feet deep down in de sand.
Hold!	on tight with both we hands.
Pull!	and tug and pull some more.
Show!	de fish who go win this war.
Crash!	We fall and de fish laughin'.
Grunt!	We up and pullin' again.
Wet!	and sandy through and through.
On no!	I wonder what Mama go do.
Look!	A big wave rollin' in.
Hurray!	Is now we bound to win!

Lynn Joseph

16

El Dorado

O the tales! The tales!
Short tales, long tales.
Ships that gleamed wood and bronze
Wide, bright sails
Waters that sparkled like crystal!

They filled our ears, heads
Our very selves.
Our hands twitching so, itching so!
Fingering the empty air
For the smooth of opal, the sharp of gold
The white weight of diamonds.

We bought the travelers rum—
Tell us more! More! More!—
Trees ringed with emeralds!
Nuggets on the shores!
Mountains brighter than the sun!
Rocks and rivers gold!

Tears salt on our faces
We boarded, stole, claimed ships
Rushed for the seas
One word on our lips—
Dorado! Dorado! Dorado!

Maggie Harris

SWIMMER

The sea swims with the dolphin
Velvet smooth splishing in
Every wave curl
Hellos an oyster from its pearl.
Watery songs tune its fin
And in the wonder of its eyes
The sea overturns the skies;
Back-stroke, front-stroke
Swirl into a butterfly-spin
And as a joke
Slants under the sea's skin;
The sea's noble prize
Rising, and plunging, higher!
The sea follows the swimming route
Licking its lips and burning water;
The dolphin's siren signals a fleet
In the coming calm of sea, neat.

Faustin Charles

SEASHELL

Shell at my ear –
come share how I hear
busy old sea in whispers.

Moans rise from ancient depths
in ocean sighs
like bands of ghost monsters.

Waves lash and fall –
in roars and a squall
with all a mystery ahhh!

James Berry

THE FRINGE OF THE SEA

We do not like to awaken
far from the fringe of the sea,
we who live upon small islands.

We like to rise up early,
quick in the agile mornings
and walk out only little distances
to look down at the water,

to know it is swaying near to us
with songs, and tides, and endless boatways,
and undulate patterns and moods.

We want to be able to saunter beside it
slowpaced in burning sunlight,
bare-armed, barefoot, bareheaded,

and to stoop down by the shallows
sifting the random water
between assaying fingers
like farmers do with soil,

and to think of turquoise mackerel
turning with consummate grace,
sleek and decorous
and elegant in high blue chambers.

We want to be able to walk out into it,
to work in it,

dive and swim and play in it,
to row and sail
and pilot over its sandless highways,
and to hear
its call and murmurs wherever we may be.

All who have lived upon small islands
want to sleep and awaken
close to the fringe of the sea.

A. L. Hendriks

AXIMU'S AWAKENING

This morning the sun
tickled my eyes
as usual

and I slid from
my hammock
and looked at the skies
as usual

I yawned and I stretched
I felt like a splash
in the cold morning water
so I made a dash
towards the path
to the sea
before Ama could call me
and give me a work.

As I burst through the bush
at the top of the hill
I froze and I shivered
my heart stood still.

Great canoes with houses
and clouds of cloth wings
hung on poles, full of wind,
strange frightening things
on the sea!

"Great Iocuhuuague Maorocon"
I whispered and knew
those terrible canoes
were coming for me.

Pamela C. Mordecai

22

OLD WORLD NEW WORLD

Spices and gold once cast a spell
on bearded men in caravels.

New World New World cried history
Old World Old World sighed every tree.

But Indian tribes long long ago
had sailed this archipelago.

They who were used to flutes of bone
translated talk of wind on stone.

Yet their feathered tongues were drowned
when Discovery beat its drum.

New World New World – spices and gold
Old World Old World – the legends told.

New World New World – cried history
Old World Old World – sighed every tree.

John Agard

CRAB MARCH

On full moon nights
the horizon eats up the sea.
Blue crabs curiously
come up from their holes,
amazed, frightened,
by the wide, empty beach
they scramble and scurry
to meet the neap surf.

Dionne Brand

Moonlight brings with it not only palm-tree shadows and ghost crabs along the shoreline. Full moon is a time for storytelling and ring-games in the yard. A time for the storyteller to invite other shadows to join the dance of fireflies in the dark – the shadows of ghosts, jumbies, duppies, call them what you will. They are as close to you as the tricky spider, Anancy. So why not stay up and listen? Make time for night-time friends.

SEE FULL MOON, HEAR JUMBIE STORY

ONE FINE DAY IN THE MIDDLE OF THE NIGHT

One fine day in the middle of the night
Two dead men began to fight
Two blind men to see fair play
One dumb man to shout hurray
A lame-foot donkey passing by
Kicked the man in he left right eye.

Traditional

I LIKE TO STAY UP

I like to stay up
and listen
when big people talking
jumbie stories

I does feel
so tingly and excited
inside me

But when my mother say
"Girl, time for bed"

Then is when
I does feel a dread

Then is when
I does jump into me bed

Then is when
I does cover up
from me feet to me head

Then is when
I does wish I didn't listen
to no stupid jumbie story

Then is when I does wish I did read
me book instead

("Jumbie" is a Guyanese word for "ghost".)

Grace Nichols

26

OBEAH ONE

Obeah One, Obeah Two,
If you don't join in,
I'll put a spell on you!
Obeah Three, Obeah Four,
I'll come knocking
With a skull on your door!
Obeah Five, Obeah Six,
My fingertips are full of tricks!
Obeah Seven, Obeah Eight,
Come and play
Before it's too late!
Obeah Nine, Obeah Ten,
Now you're the Witch,
Let's start again!

Vyanne Samuels

BANYAN TREE

Moonshine tonight, come mek we dance an sing,
Moonshine tonight, come mek we dance an sing.
Me deh rock so, yu deh rock so, under banyan tree,
Me deh rock so, yu deh rock so, under banyan tree.

Ladies mek curtsy, an gentlemen mek bow,
Ladies mek curtsy, an gentlemen mek bow.
Me deh rock so, yu deh rock so, under banyan tree,
Me deh rock so, yu deh rock so, under banyan tree.

Den we join hans and dance aroun an roun,
Den we join hans and dance aroun an roun.
Me deh rock so, yu deh rock so, under banyan tree,
Me deh rock so, yu deh rock so, under banyan tree.

Traditional

DUPPY DAN

Duppy Dan
aint no livin man

Duppy Dan
done dead an gone

Duppy Dan
nah have foot

Duppy Dan
nah have hand

Yet Duppy Dan cross water
Duppy Dan cross land

Duppy Dan ride white horse
pon pitchdark night

Run like-a-hell stranger
when Duppy Dan tell you goodnight

John Agard

JUMBIE MAN

Jumbie man returning red
Fire bleeding the dead;
With his see-through head
Walking where angels fear to tread.
Jumbie man turning day into night
Giving all man-jack a fright;

His front teeth spinning out
And jawbones jumping about;
Drinking blood mix with rum,
When you tease him for some
He'll shout:
"I'll strike you deaf and dumb!"

Faustin Charles

31

EBBEELEEWEE

Ebbeeleewee
Must be
The thinnest man
You'll ever see.
Sideways he's invisible;
He can sleep under a razor blade
Giving shade
To a mosquito's bubble.
He can go through hairline cracks
Slipping between thumb and thumbtacks.
In a gentle breeze
He disappears with ease.
When he eats and drink,
No one knows where the food goes;
It makes you think
His belly must be in his toes.

Faustin Charles

32

ANANCY

Anancy is a trickster of no small order
half a man and half a spider
Miss Muffet was sure glad
he hadn't sat beside her

He's unlike any of your friends
He's a whole lot smarter
He tricks and he outsmarts
He's a real fast talker

He's slow on his feet
a zip on his wit
When it comes to thinking quick
he's a wizard at tricks

He's never lost a game
'cause he cheats, double-crosses his friends
When he can't win fair
he's a spider again

Anancy is a trickster of no small order
half a man and half a spider
Miss Muffet was sure glad
he hadn't sat beside her

Lillian Allen

MAMA-WATA

Down by the seaside
when the moon is in bloom
sits Mama-Wata
gazing up at the moon

She sits as she combs
her hair like a loom
she sits as she croons
a sweet kind of tune

But don't go near Mama-Wata
when the moon is in bloom
for sure she will take you
down to your doom.

Grace Nichols

JAMAICAN SONG

Little toad little toad mind yourself
mind yourself let me plant my corn
plant my corn to feed my horse
feed my horse to run my race –
the sea is full of more than I know
moon is bright like night-time sun
night is dark like all eyes shut
    Mind – mind yu not harmed
    somody know bout yu
    somody know bout yu

Little toad little toad mind yourself
mind yourself let me build my house
build my house to be at home
be at home till I one day vanish –
the sea is full of more than I know
moon is bright like night-time sun
night is dark like all eyes shut
    Mind – mind yu not harmed
    somody know bout yu
    somody know bout yu

James Berry

Have you ever tried listening to the land? Every land speaks with many tongues, whether it's the whisper of a tree, the rush of a waterfall, or the roar of a hurricane. Listen to the land breathing as to your own heartbeat. Let your ears tune in to the call of the six-o'clock bee and the pung-la-la chorus of frogs, not to mention that unforgettable Soca beat.

LISTENING TO THE LAND

PROVERB

Bush have ears
Bush have eyes

Traditional

LISTEN

Shhhhhhhhhhhhhhhhhhhhhhhhhhh!
Sit still, very still
And listen.
Listen to wings
Lighter than eyelashes
Stroking the air.
Know what the thin breeze
Whispers on high
To the coconut trees.
Listen and hear.

Telcine Turner

WHO U?

Who U? Who U?
the little Bird cries.
DUDDUP on the left
DUDDUP on the right
Paddle on, a canoe replies.

Who U? Who U?
the little Bird cries.
Clack Clack Clack
says tall bamboo
living in Bamboo Walk.

Who U? Who U?
the little Bird cries.
Osso Rorro Osso Rorro
Roaring water Roaring water
says river rushing by.

Who U? Who U?
the little Bird cries.
OUUMMMM Ouummmm
chants big Baboon
Rain caller is my name.

Who U? Who U?
the little Bird cries.
Tatata tap tatata tap
tiny feet of rain dance
answer on rooftop.

Who U? Who U?
the little Bird cries.
Listen with care
and you will hear
all the jungle creatures
give their reply.

Marc Matthews

39

COCONUT GROOVE

At the coconut groove
See everybody move,
They boogie together
Despite the weather.
It's raining, it's blowing
But the rhythm is flowing,
As the frog from France
With agouti breakdance.
Frisky mongoose
Lets it all hang loose,
While the slippery snake
Does the S-bend shake.
With the monkeys on drums
The humming-birds hum.
The music's so good
Down here in the woods.
Juicy Miss Mango
Does a daring tango
With Mr Jackfruit
In his fine green suit.
The potatoes look sweet
As they bop to the beat,
As everybody swings
And does their thing
Down at the coconut groove.

Anne Marie Linden

NATURE

We have neither Summer nor Winter
Neither Autumn nor Spring.
We have instead the days
When the gold sun shines on the lush green canefields –
Magnificently.
The days when the rain beats like bullets on the roofs
And there is no sound but the swish of water in the gullies
And trees struggling in the high Jamaica winds.
Also there are the days when leaves fade from off guango trees
And the reaped canefields lie bare and fallow to the sun.
But best of all there are the days when the mango and the
    logwood blossom,
When the bushes are full of the sound of bees and the scent
    of honey,
When the tall grass sways and shivers to the slightest breath
    of air,
When the buttercups have paved the earth with yellow stars,
And beauty comes suddenly and the rains have gone.

H. D. Carberry

HUMMING-BIRD

Humming-bird, humming-bird, why don't you hum?
I do not hum because I am dumb.
Then why are you called humming-bird of all things?
Because of the noise I make with my wings.

Odette Thomas

RACK-A-BYE, BABY

Rack-a-bye, baby, pon tap a tree tap,
 Wen de win blow de crib a go swing;
Wen de lim bruck de crib a go drap,
 Den lim, crib, an baby, eberyting drap. BRAP!

Louise Bennett

43

LISTENING TO THE LAND

That night when I left you on the bridge
I bent down
kneeling on my knee
and pressed my ear to listen to the land.

I bent down
listening to the land
but all I heard was tongueless whispering.

On my right hand was the sea behind the wall
the sea that has no business in the forest
and I bent down
listening to the land
and all I heard was tongueless whispering
as if some buried slave wanted to speak again.

Martin Carter

LISTENING FOR ANSWERS

Why do birds fly?
Why is the sky blue?
Why do cats purr?
And why is the truth true?

Why all these questions?
Why such a task?
I want the answers
But who do I ask?

My mother, my father
My sisters don't know.
They can't find answers
They've searched high and low.

So I guess I'll just sit here
And rattle my brain
And hope all the answers
Fall down with the rain.

Aimee Harris-Watmore

TELL ME TREES!
WHAT ARE YOU WHISPERING?

It is strange
Standing here
Beneath the whispering trees
Far away from the haunts of men.
Tell me trees!
What are you whispering?

When I am dead
I shall come and lie
Beneath your fallen leaves...
But tell me trees!
What are you whispering?

They shall bury me
Beneath your fallen leaves.
My robe shall be
Green, fallen leaves.
My love shall be
Fresh, fallen leaves.
My lips shall kiss
Sweet, fallen leaves.
I and the leaves shall lie together
Never parting...
I and the leaves shall always lie together
And know no parting.

It is so strange
Standing here
Beneath the whispering trees!
Tell me trees!
What are you whispering?

Wilson Harris

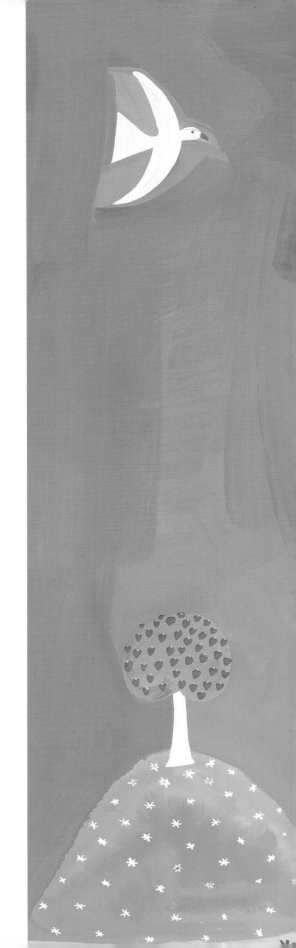

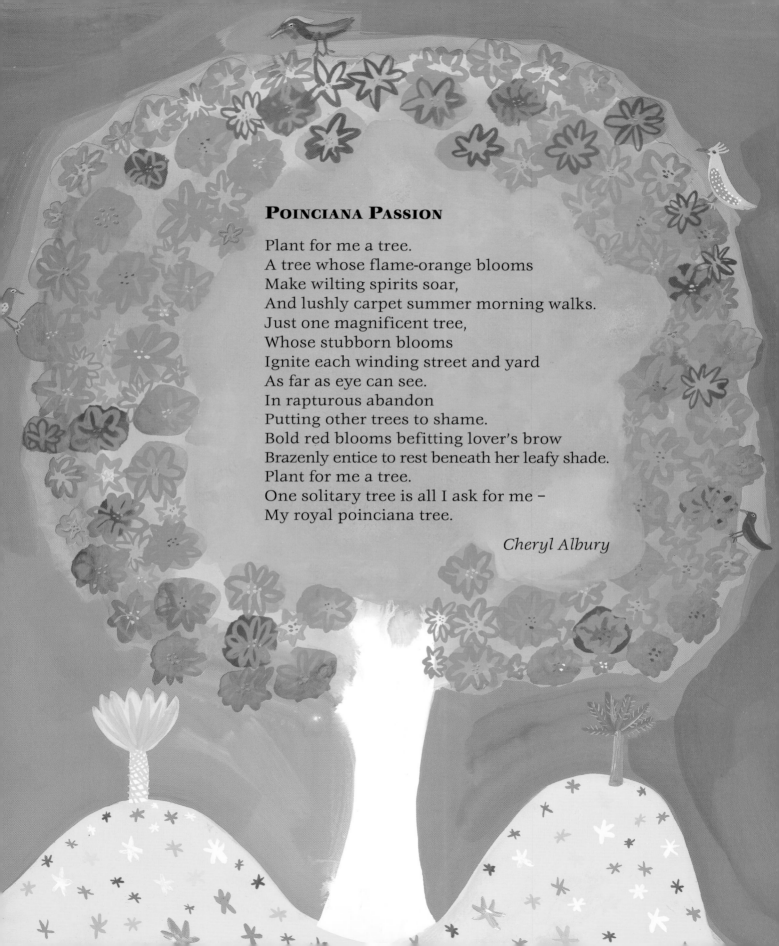

POINCIANA PASSION

Plant for me a tree.
A tree whose flame-orange blooms
Make wilting spirits soar,
And lushly carpet summer morning walks.
Just one magnificent tree,
Whose stubborn blooms
Ignite each winding street and yard
As far as eye can see.
In rapturous abandon
Putting other trees to shame.
Bold red blooms befitting lover's brow
Brazenly entice to rest beneath her leafy shade.
Plant for me a tree.
One solitary tree is all I ask for me –
My royal poinciana tree.

Cheryl Albury

SIX O'CLOCK FEELING

You ever feel
dat six o'clock feeling
six o'clock shadow falling
wrappin you up
mekking you stop
an tink
bout all dese tings
God doin
six o'clock bee calling
All dem tree
tekking strange, strange shape
an stan up
sharp! sharp! gainst dat sky
You know dem six o'clock colour
pink an orange an blue an purple an black

dat six o'clock feeling
mekking you feel like touchin
mekking you feel so small
you could cry
or fall down pun you knee
and thank God
you could still
see He six o'clock sky

Kamal Singh

NIGHT SONGS

"Pung-la-la," from the frog by my window.
"Shirr-ooo-ooo," from the midnight manicou.
"Ba-lo-ma," from the agouti in the yard.
"Rill-dee-dee," from the mongoose in the tree.
"Gonck-gonck," from the tatou by the pole.
"Urol-el-el," from the matapel.
"Goodnight," I whisper to my moonlight friends
  singing their bedtime songs to the sky.

Lynn Joseph

Someone once said that the way to a people's heart is through their food and folksongs. And you couldn't make a better start than at a market bustling with smells, colours and voices. "Today is pumpkin birthday, pumpkin giving away," cries one trader. "Coconut water good for yuh daughter," cries another. The sound of words. The flavour of foods. The quiet reflection of fruits in a bowl, tempting eyes to feast and tongues to taste.

COME TASTE AND BUY

CARIBBEAN PROVERB

Don't spread tablecloth till pot done boil.

Traditional

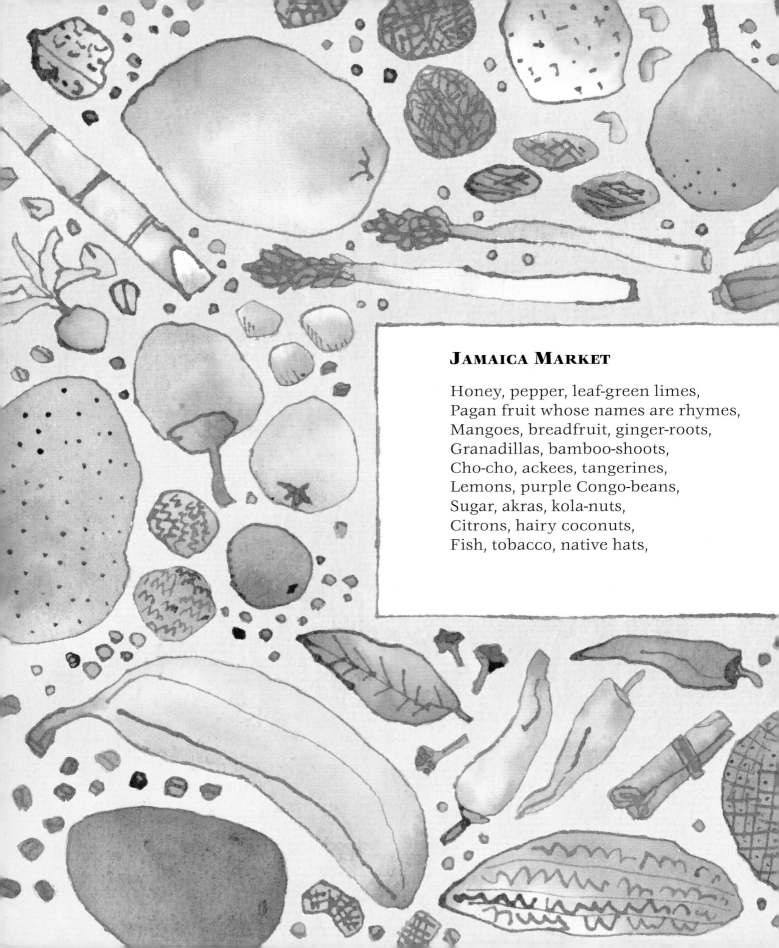

JAMAICA MARKET

Honey, pepper, leaf-green limes,
Pagan fruit whose names are rhymes,
Mangoes, breadfruit, ginger-roots,
Granadillas, bamboo-shoots,
Cho-cho, ackees, tangerines,
Lemons, purple Congo-beans,
Sugar, akras, kola-nuts,
Citrons, hairy coconuts,
Fish, tobacco, native hats,

Gold bananas, woven mats,
Plantains, wild-thyme, pallid leeks,
Pigeons with their scarlet beaks,
Oranges and saffron yams,
Baskets, ruby guava jams,
Turtles, goat-skins, cinnamon,
Allspice, conch-shells, golden rum.
Black skins, babel – and the sun
That burns all colours into one.

Agnes Maxwell-Hall

COCONUT WOMAN

Coconut Woman is calling out
And every day you can hear her shout,
Coconut Woman is calling out
And every day you can hear her shout –
    Get your coconut water, *four for five*
    Man it's good for your daughter, *four for five*
    Coco got a lotta iron, *four for five*
    Make you strong like a lion, *four for five*.

A lady tell me the other day
No one can take her sweet man away.
I ask her what was the mystery,
She say coconut water and rice curry.
    You can cook it in a pot, *four for five*
    You can serve it very hot, *four for five*
    Coco got a lotta iron, *four for five*
    Make you strong like a lion, *four for five*.

Coconut Woman say you'll agree
Coconut make very nice candy,
The thing that's best if you're feeling glum
Is coconut water with a little rum.
    It could make you very tipsy, *four for five*
    Make you feel very frisky, *four for five*
    Coco got a lotta iron, *four for five*
    Make you strong like a lion, *four for five*.

Harry Belafonte and Irving Burgie

I LOVE JOHNNIE BAKE

I love Johnnie bake,
I love Johnnie bake.
My mout water
wen I think of Johnnie bake
I in de kitchen
wen Granma make Johnnie bake.

Wen she grate coconut
to put in Johnnie bake
I eat de sweet, sweet bits
too small to grate.
She warn meh about belly-ache;
but I cahn help it,
I really love Johnnie bake.

She kneading de flour
an she whole body shake.
I near de oven,
where she bake Johnnie bake,
looking at how she cuff
de dough flat;
and I cahn get enough
of Johnnie bake.
Nothing new!
I love Johnnie bake!
I LOVE JOHNNIE BAKE!

John Lyons

56

DUMPLINS

"Janey, you see nobody pass here?"
    "No, me friend."
"Sarah, you see nobody pass here?"
    "No, me friend."
"Well, one of me dumplins gone."
    "Don't tell me so!"
"One of me dumplins gone."

"Janey, you see nobody pass here?"
    "No, me friend."
"Sarah, you see nobody pass here?"
    "No, me friend."
"Well, two of me dumplins gone."
    "Don't tell me so!"
"Two of me dumplins gone."

Traditional

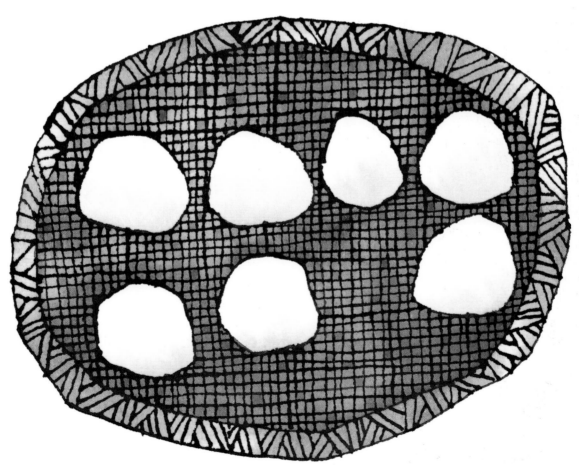

HUNGRY GIRL

"Tell me, please tell me Mummy,
  Why the strange noises in my tummy?"

"Well, my little Dumplin Head,
  your tummy is asking to be fed;

  not with fatty crisps and sweets,
  but with rice and peas and spicy meats;

  and with your appetite of late,
  I am sure you'll polish-lick your plate."

John Lyons

GUIDANCE

Wash yuh han' dem before yuh eat,
Sit still, teck yuh foot dem off the seat,
Don' scrape the plate with yuh knife an' fork,
An' keep quiet when big people a-talk,
Stop drag yuh foot dem pon the floor,
Ah tell yuh a'ready, don' slam the door,
Cover up yuh mout' when yuh a-cough,
Don' be greedy, give yuh sister half
O' the banana that yuh eatin' there,
What kind o'dress that yuh a-wear?
Don' kiss yuh teeth when me talk to yuh,
An' mind how yuh lookin' at me too,
Teck me good advice, me girl,
Manners carry yuh through the worl',
Ah tellin' yuh all this fe yuh own good,
Yuh should thank me, show some gratitude.

Life is very tough for me,
When Uncle Henry comes to tea.

Valerie Bloom

FRUIT IN A BOWL

Fruit in a bowl.

Full goldenapples with veined skins so fine
That just a look might burst them –

                tangerines
For all the world like small green solid bells
Promising little kisses of astringency.

Yellow bananas, cool and firm to feel
Lying in curves of silken-tongued delight.

And great plumpted mangoes, sweetness
    to the seed.
Huge cut pawpaws bearing dark-seedling cargoes.

And sapodillas with their sweet, brown kernels
Aching to change to sugar once again.

Tropical fruit.

A. J. Seymour

THE PAWPAW

Four little boys, tattered,
Fingers and faces splattered
With mud, had climbed
In the rain and caught
A pawpaw which they brought,
Like a bomb, to my house. I saw
Them coming: a serious, mumbling,
Tumbling bunch who stopped
At the steps in a hunch.
Releasing the fruit from the leaf
It was wrapped in, I watched them
Carefully wash the pawpaw
Like a nugget of gold. This done,
With rainwater, till it shone
They climbed into the house
To present the present to me.
A mocking sign of the doom of all flesh?
Or the purest gold in the kingdom?

Kamau Braithwaite

PINEAPPLE

Pineapple.
Prickly,
Pungent,
Picked for
Sweetness and juice.
Yellow rings
On my finger,
Chunks of yellow,
Drips of sun,
Pineapple, under
A golden one.

Vyanne Samuels

Journeying across unknown seas has had a pull on human beings all over the world since time began. And Caribbean peoples have had their share of journeying across the globe. One famous ship called "Windrush" arrived with Caribbean pioneers at Tilbury Docks in England in 1948. But the Caribbean presence goes back much further, and people of Caribbean ancestry have settled all over the world. And so the sea continues to write its history. And as the Caribbean lady says in the poem, "Wherever there's God's earth, I'm at home."

WINDRUSH CHILD

ABNA BABNA

Abna Babna
Lady-Snee
Ocean potion
Sugar and tea
Potato roast
And English toast
Out goes she.

Traditional

WINDRUSH CHILD

Behind you
Windrush child
palm trees wave goodbye

above you
Windrush child
seabirds asking why

around you
Windrush child
blue water rolling by

beside you
Windrush child
your Windrush mum and dad

think of storytime yard
and mango mornings

and new beginnings
doors closing and opening

will things turn out right?
At least the ship will arrive
in midsummer light

and you Windrush child
think of Grandmother
telling you don't forget to write

and with one last hug
walk good walk good
and the sea's wheel carries on spinning

and from that place England
you tell her in a letter
of your Windrush adventure

stepping in a big ship
not knowing how long the journey
or that you're stepping into history

bringing your Caribbean eye
to another horizon
Grandmother's words your shining beacon

learning how to fly
the kite of your dreams
in an English sky

Windrush child
walking good walking good
in a mind-opening
meeting of snow and sun

John Agard

64

I LOVE ME MUDDER...

I love me mudder and me mudder love me
we come so far over de sea,
we heard dat de streets were paved with gold
sometime it hot sometime it cold,
I love me mudder and me mudder love me
we try fe live in harmony
you might know her as Valerie
but to me she is my mummy.

She shouts at me daddy so loud some time
she don't smoke weed she don't drink wine
she always do the best she can
she work damn hard down ina England,
she's always singing some kind of song
she have very big muscles and she very very strong
she likes pussy-cats and she love cashew nuts
she don't bother with no ifs or buts.

I love me mudder and me mudder love me
we come so far over de sea,
we heard dat de streets were paved with gold
sometime it hot sometime it cold,
I love her and she love me too
and dis is a love I know is true
me and my mudder we love you too.

Benjamin Zephaniah

MY GRAN VISITS ENGLAND

My Gran was a Caribbean lady
As Caribbean as could be
She came across to visit us
In Shoreham by the sea.

She'd hardly put her suitcase down
When she began a digging spree
Out in the back garden
To see what she could see

And she found:
That the ground was as groundy
That the frogs were as froggy
That the earthworms were as worthy

That the weeds were as weedy
That the seeds were as seedy
That the bees were as busy
As those back home

And she paused from her digging
And she wondered
And she looked at her spade
And she pondered

Then she stood by a rose
As a slug passed by her toes
And she called to my dad
As she struck pose after pose,

"Boy, come and take my photo – the place cold,
But wherever there's God's earth, I'm at home."

Grace Nichols

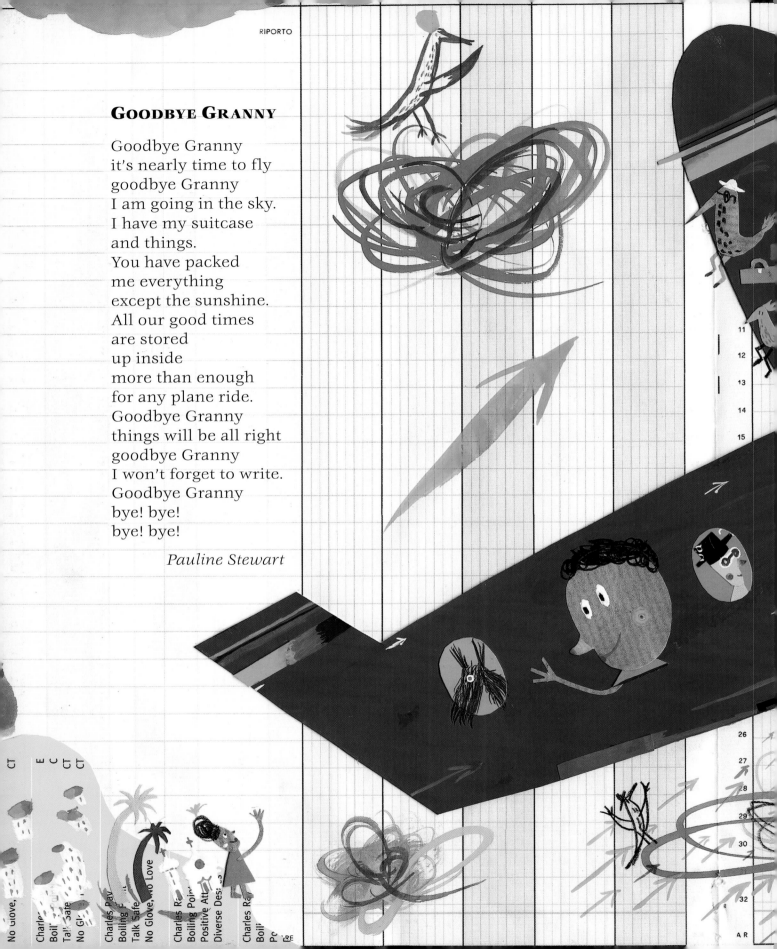

GOODBYE GRANNY

Goodbye Granny
it's nearly time to fly
goodbye Granny
I am going in the sky.
I have my suitcase
and things.
You have packed
me everything
except the sunshine.
All our good times
are stored
up inside
more than enough
for any plane ride.
Goodbye Granny
things will be all right
goodbye Granny
I won't forget to write.
Goodbye Granny
bye! bye!
bye! bye!

Pauline Stewart

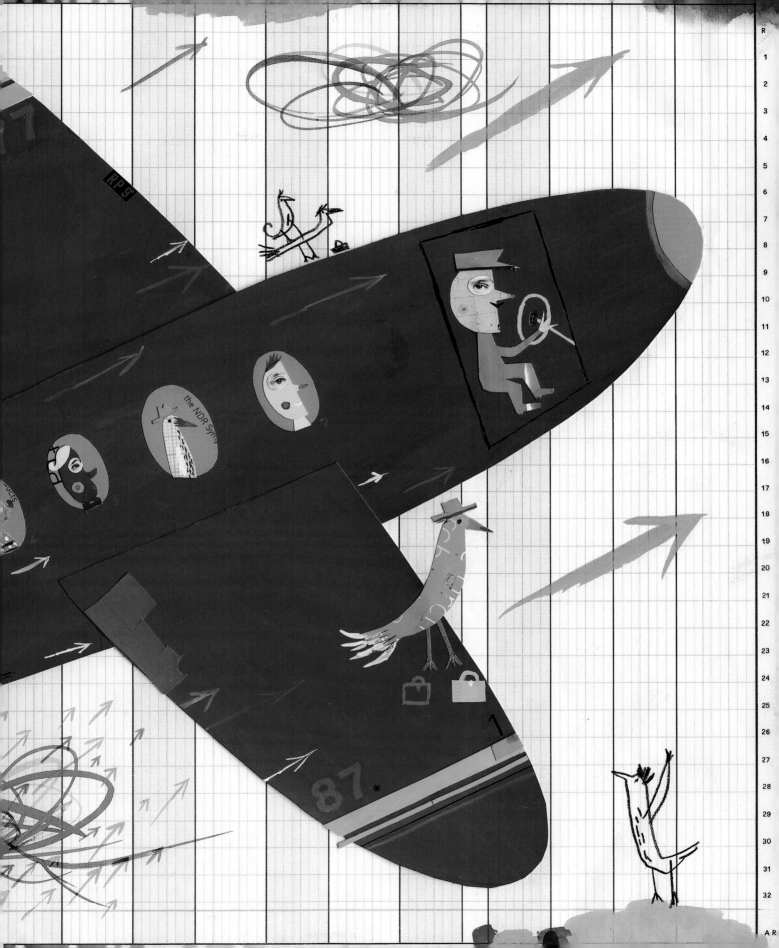

DE

De snow, de sleet, de lack o'heat,
De wishy-washy sunlight,
De lip turn blue, de cold, "ACHOO!"
De runny nose, de frostbite,

De creakin' knee, de misery,
De joint dem all rheumatic,
De icy bed (de blanket dead),
De burs' pipe in de attic.

De window a-shake, de glass near break,
De wind dat cut like razor,
De wonderin' why you never buy
De window from dat double-glazer.

De heavy coat, zip to de throat,
De nose an' ears all pinky,
De weepin' sky, de clothes can't dry,
De day dem long an' inky.

De icy road, de heavy load,
De las' minute Christmas shoppin'
De cuss an' fret 'cause you feget
De ribbon an' de wrappin'.

De mud, de grime, de slush, de slime,
De place gloomy since November,
De sinkin' heart is jus' de start, o'
De wintertime,
December.

Valerie Bloom

MAKING MY FIRST SNOWMAN IN MY MOTHER'S PINK RUBBER GLOVES

I scooped and shaped him lovingly,
I piled and patted best as could be,
though my pink hands were burning me,
I kept on building my first snowman.

I shaped his shoulders and fixed his neck,
I smoothed his face and rounded his head,
though my pink hands were freezing me,
I kept on building my first snowman.

I put the usual carrot in, for the nose,
a banana for a mouth, my two best conkers
for his eyes,
though my pink hands were killing me,
I kept on building my first snowman.

I threw my dad's black jacket
to keep the cold from his back,
I stuck on his head the old felt hat,
then I stepped back.

Why was he staring at me with those big eyes?
Why was he so freezingly alive?
Man, why was he looking at me so?
                    Oh, no,

He wasn't a snowman.
HE WAS A SNOWCROW!

Grace Nichols

THE NAMES THAT RAN AWAY

First it was Nana Bonso Prempeh that dropped to the floor.
Next thing you know, that name was out of the door.
Swimming with beads across the water,
at home as a hippo in the River Volta.

And before I could say Gustavus Vassa,
another name was off skipping and scooting.
There, kicking legs over the Elba,
none other than Vladimir Poplocovitch Anatoli Putin.

One by one these names come stumbling out,
some heading north, some heading south.
Soon, Dayanand Sarawati Gupta-Gupta
was slithering down the Ganges for Calcutta.

O Yo-Yo Yahn-Yahn Ah Ming,
why do you leave me here standing,
while over the Yellow River you fly
like a swallow on the way to Peking?

Come back, come back, don't run away.
For some reason or other, the names won't stay.
My tongue keeps twisting, my mouth goes dry,
but not one of them hears my cry.

The names have gone too far from me.
Where's Tobias Henry Burlington of Surrey?
O I should have guessed. Wriggling down the Thames.
Following the steps of all those other names.

Kwame Dawes

OCCASION

Music bites them,
stings them.
Everybody moves
the room of break-up body shapes

in some steady bluejeaned rock
some fat and thin shin kicks
some crazy and cool breakdance
some push-push and a prance
easy and stiff kind of swing
some wild-hair head spin
lots of busy twists
in the rave-up like happy fits.

Legs the scissors cutting
arms the wings flying
hips the snakes in a wiggle
O some bodies get in a muddle.

Rhythm grabs them swamped.
Girls leap, boys leap; they stamp.
They rock it, they break it.
They everything it
with everything one say –
today's a celebration day!

James Berry

Index of Poets and First Lines

WALKER BOOKS is the world's leading
independent publisher of children's books.
Working with the best authors and illustrators
we create books for all ages, from babies
to teenagers – books your child will
grow up with and always remember. So…

FOR THE BEST CHILDREN'S BOOKS,
LOOK FOR THE BEAR